Starting Over @ 69

The Natural Law of Attraction in Action

Jon Rhodie

Published by Clink Street Publishing 2022

ISBN: 978-1-915229-82-3
eISBN: 978-1-915229-83-0

Chapter 1

69. This is a true story. At this age we hope to be living in our own comfortable mortgage free home and have a good pension to live on. We envisage being able to travel abroad to destinations we have only seen on TV, or just create a garden, or sit down and read all the books we have ever intended to read.

BUT! Sometimes life can take an unexpected sharp left turn, and suddenly we find ourselves on an unfamiliar road, heading in a direction that is unknown to us, and going where we do not want to go in life. The signposts all point in the direction of *The Valley of the Shadow*, and your life is turned upside down! Dramatic as this may sound it is an experience common to man. As common as flu, and there are a countless number of people in the world today experiencing extreme, and often abusive, hardships after their lives have taken that sudden sharp left turn, and you can't just turn around and go back the way you came. The reason for writing this book is to show that you can make it through *The Valley of the Shadow* if you employ the principles laid out here. They are tried and tested, and if they worked for me and countless others, *then why not for you?*

This sudden unexpected left turn can be caused by a hurtful disappointment, the failure of your business, a romantic affaire gone wrong, a failed marriage, or cruel physical or mental abuse such as incest, rape or other abuse, which can leave a person scarred for life. The list is endless. But possibly the hardest to bear is bereavement. The loss of your soulmate which knocks all wind out of your sails and plunges you into black depression. The death of a parent, your first born, or the loss of a favourite aunt or friend, I'm sure you know what I mean, and you are heading down a slippery slope, down a rocky road fit only for a 4x4 into the dark foreboding muddy *Valley of the Shadow.* The Good Book calls it 'the valley of the shadow of death', but we will keep it just to The Valley of the Shadow.

Yet, in the Good Book it says, "Though I walk ***THROUGH*** the Valley," and one needs to keep that uppermost in your mind, there is a way through! Regardless of your circumstances! The floor of the Valley is littered with the bleached bones of those who have decided that the way is too hard, and have given up, and it is hard! No doubt about it! They simply didn't know how to navigate their way THROUGH the Valley and have no one to guide them. Others are trapped among the rocks in vexation of spirit like the strange creature Sméagol in Middle Earth of the Hobbits' tale, ever searching for that something precious they have lost – and cannot find it again. People just don't know how to handle you when you are going through the Valley. They cannot begin to understand the emotions you are experiencing, and few people are trained to deal with this. So, they turn away and ignore you, saying, "Pull yourself together, Man!" They cannot deal with your problems, so they brush them aside and detach themselves from them. People who sympathetically say, "I know *exactly* how you feel," really do not have the faintest idea of how you feel. Because they have never been where you are! In many cases, when faced with difficult circumstances in life you can apply the simple philosophy of, *'This too shall pass!'* The storms of life will pass, and many problems will resolve themselves. But! Others drag you down into The Valley of the Shadow, and into the depths of despair, from which there seems to be no way out!

A man once discovered a very rich reef of gold which he mined and became very wealthy. But suddenly one day he lost the reef! Millennia before the Earth had shifted, and although he knew geographically where the reef should be, where it had moved to, he dug and dug until he had exhausted his finances, and he sold the mine for a song, convinced he would never find the reef again. The new owner dug down *three feet* – and hit the gold reef again! Today this is still one of the richest gold mines in South Africa! Don't give up! You may be only three feet from the gold! *'Be bold, and unseen forces will come to your aid.'*

Yes, I have been through the Valley, several times, and each time I have learned something new about how to cope. Times of depression since childhood, booze addiction which I had to overcome, bereavement twice not counting my parents, and a broken second marriage, plus many disappointments along the way. They say you find your heaven or your hell in the one you marry. My first wife, my soulmate, was heaven. The second one was… Often the left turn happens gradually. Without even noticing it you begin to drift off the main highway on to a secondary road. Gradually the road descends and begins to deteriorate until you find your life spiralling down out of control into confusion and heartache, and you don't know where to turn next. Your vehicle runs out of road and gets wrecked, and you find yourself on foot up to your knees in foul smelling mud! The Scribes and Pharisees walk past on the other side saying, "Oh shame!" and offer help that never comes! Here you need to understand that *If nothing changes, then, nothing changes, and everything remains the same.'* Read that again. Here-in lays the first secret of getting out of the Valley by using the Law of Attraction.

If you are in the same position today as you were in a year ago, then you are likely to be in exactly the same position as you are in now in a year's time – two years – five years. Nothing will change! Ask yourself the question, 'Is this what I want for my life?' Something has got to change in order to get out of the Valley. Sometimes that change is thrust upon us by circumstances, but more often YOU have got to make that change! I have met many people who do not want that change, because their current situation gets them lots of attention and sympathy, and they thrive on that and crave it like a drug! A woman once told her friends, "The doctor says I am very, very, sick! He says I am suffering from hypochondria." This is not a quick-fix solution that you can *try* to see if it works. You have got to want that change more than life itself! You have got to determine in your mind, "I refuse to live like this! I WILL rise above where I am today!" Say those words out loud, now! This requires work and commitment on your part!

I don't know exactly where my last left turn began. I was still living in South Africa at the time. I had gone through a very rough time for seven years after my first wife's passing eight days into the new millennium, sinking down into manic depression. She was my soulmate. My mental health suffered badly. This was a sudden left turn, and it took all the wind out of my sails. The first evening when all the well-wishers had left and I was alone, I sat alone on the edge of our double bed with my .38 Spl. revolver in my hand and said, 'God! Give me just ONE reason why I should carry on living!' and a strong thought instantly came into my mind. 'Your daughter.' I knew then that I could not burden my remaining daughter with the death of both her parents within eight hours of each other. I considered this for a while and said, 'OK. I will live.' And put the gun away. I existed. Although it was like being shot into outer darkness, into a void, where there was no light, no sound, no direction, and nothing to comfort the cries from my heart. I simply existed until time healed the wounds, and that took seven years! During that time, I just let people walk all over me and didn't care. There are those who took full advantage of this and unashamedly stole my possessions.

Nine years after my wife's passing, I was living in a nice ground floor flat attached to a house in a pleasant quiet neighbourhood in Durban, South Africa. I had a good pension to live on, and I was actively involved in a church. Life was going well again. But then after a season it all began to gradually slip and slide and spiral downhill out of control again. This left turn was largely due to my own wrong choice. A wrong decision which I knew was wrong at the time, but I did nothing to change it. Thus began the last trip down into The Valley of the Shadow, and into the extraordinary journey I went on after that to when I came out of the Valley again. Today I am living in England, and at this time of writing I have enough to be content with. I have a nice flat to live in, and enough money to live on with a little to spare. Besides that, I am living my lifelong dream of becoming a full-time artist, and I happily paint pictures all day. Life is good again. But if I had not made the change, I would not be where I am today. I would still be where I was, because nothing would have changed!

The descent into The Valley

To understand where I am today, I need to take you back to where it possibly all started. I had been on my own for nine years and desperately wanted someone to love. In those nine years I had two romantic encounters with women. Both ended in disaster and vexation of spirit. Now I met a lady who seemed to tick all the boxes. Intellectually and spiritually, we seemed to be on the same page and feelings of affection soon began to grow. After a good few months, we decided to tie the knot. Now, from the outset I want to say I do not lay the blame at the feet of the lady concerned for what happened in the next four years to come. That responsibility lays firmly on my own shoulders because I made a wrong decision. You are responsible for your own life and all the decisions you make in it. If your business fails because your partner ran away with all the money, that is your responsibility! You chose the wrong partner! Learn from it and don't make the same mistake again next time.

It all boils down to just one thing. Her zodiac sign is Scorpio and mine is Sagittarius, and they don't mix! They are like oil and water. They are a very bad combination of the zodiac signs. The fact is, I knew this before we got involved, and I chose to ignore it! I also noticed she had a sharp tongue, but surely, she wouldn't use it on me if she loved me, or so I thought. I let my heart rule my head, and it was to my detriment. Immediately I can hear some of you say, "I don't believe in that junk!" Or "That's not Scriptural! Zodiac is evil, it's of the Devil!" (or so they say). Well maybe you need to do your own research on the subject, and not just blindly accept what other people, or the church, says. You can find it all in the Good Book. Who flung the Milky Way and the rest of the stars into space, and what were they intended for? Start with creation and see what it says.

Not all marriages are made in heaven, as we are led to believe. The majority are our own choice, and I made the wrong choice! Scorpio loves to be in charge and to dominate. That's why they have two big pinchers and a sting in their tail. However, Sagittarius, the centaur, half man, half wild stallion, refuses to be fenced in or controlled. They are a free spirit. They have four hooves that can kick and cut, and they are armed with a bow and arrow to boot! Annoy the centaur too much and you will get a good swift kick, or they will pull out an arrow and nail you to the wall, or simply turn and gallop off into the distance out of range. Each star sign has its own personality traits, and Scorpio and Sag' are incompatible. This marriage was doomed from the beginning! She was just being a Scorpio and I was just being a Sagittarian.

At first it was all love and roses, then the honeymoon was over, and the fighting began. After about two months of marriage the first serious fight erupted. I was unhappy about the amount of time she spent on her laptop each evening after she came home from work, as I wanted more quality time with my new bride. I was already retired and home alone all day and she would be on her laptop from five in the evening till nine pm at night and then go to bed, while I sat and twiddled my thumbs in isolation. That laptop put a wall between us. The battle for who wears the pants had begun. When I confronted her, she defended her position saying that is what she had always done to relax, and suddenly she made out like it was all MY fault! Scorpio loves to be in control. This was unfamiliar territory to me as I hate fighting and had not experienced it in my first marriage, and I was caught on the back foot defending myself. When I continued to press home my argument, I found out she had come into the marriage with a back door still open. This was, 'Well, if this doesn't work, I'll just pack my bags and leave!'

When it was obvious the lady was not going to win, she used this as a weapon and threw down the gauntlet. "Well, if you don't like it, I'll just…!" I was shocked. This was no way to build a new marriage, and it was the last thing I wanted! So, I backed down.

Time went by and everything was cool, till another argument erupted some months later. Again, she defended herself and laid all the blame on me. This time she subjected me to a whole range or rapid-fire accusations which were untrue, or just plain designed to hurt and cut, and which sent me reeling. No sooner had I started to defend myself against one untrue accusation when another one was fired at me, and then another, until I lost track and my head was spinning. The one I do remember because it was so laughable was that I had only married her so I could have her as a sex slave! **HULLOW!** If I had wanted a sex slave I would be thinking more like, um, 22, than a middle-aged woman with a mature figure! Again, she used her 'Get Out of Jail Free' card and threatened to leave. And again, I backed down, and an uneasy peace was restored. But now I could see a pattern of behaviour emerging. Always pay attention to patterns of behaviour.

In the timeline of things about two years had elapsed. During that time other things started to go bad. Suddenly I lost my pension due to some administrative error, and it was not an easy thing to get sorted out as the pension came from overseas, and I would have to go there to fix it. This caused me a lot of distress and anxiety. Now we were dependant on her salary and another small South African government pension I had, which wouldn't buy you a week's groceries. Money began to get tight. I never knew what she earned, but at the end of the month there was often very little in her account. I presumed she had other debts she was paying off. Yet whenever she needed money, she would just go off to the loan shark, and borrow some more! Many times, we had to resort to taking things down to the pawn shop just to put food on the table. Just as many times we didn't have the money to redeem them, and over time we lost almost all the things of value to us.

Still reeling from that blow, we were soon hit by another. The sheriff of the court appeared at our door one morning to tell us the property we lived on had been repossessed by the bank! The owner had abandoned it, and he lived overseas. Ourselves, and the occupants of the house, were ordered to move out and the electricity was cut off. Everything was spiralling down into a vortex of sticky mud in the bottom of The Valley of the Shadow.

We simply did not have the money to move! So, for the next two years we illegally squatted on the premises with no electricity and very little water. The municipality cut the water down to a trickle to try and force us out because the lights and water bill had mounted up very high, and that was the responsibility of the owner. We offered to pay, but the house was not registered in our name so they wouldn't allow it. Out of necessity, each time they came and switched off the electricity at the meter box outside and put their seal on it, I would wait until they left and go and cut their seal and switch the electricity back on! Desperate times require desperate measures. Eventually they climbed the pole in the street and cut the electricity wires to the property. Now we had to resort to using paraffin lamps and boiling pots of water on a gas cooker to get four inches of water to bath in, and then we shared the water! The occupants of the house were also in financial distress and also squatted in the house, and there we stayed until the property came up for auction two years later. All this stress also played havoc with our relationship and fights over money were common.

A year into this unpleasant situation a major fight erupted, over what I can't remember. It was a real verbal knock down drag out fight with no holds barred, and the sting of the scorpion came into play. Their sting is in their tongue, and I was subject to a tongue-lashing that left me very, very angry for days. Scorpio can assassinate your entire character with the sting of their tongue, while you try desperately to defend yourself. Forget it mate, you just can't win! The family in the house overheard the entire fight and the man came to me next morning and his sympathy was with me. He said to me, "That was untrue. Unnecessary, and uncalled for!" Any respect they had for my wife after that went straight out the door! Of course, the lady had used her weapon and threatened to move out. But this time I was very angry and turned to her and said, "Well if that's the way you feel! Pack your bags and *F*** off!*" I had had enough! I remember the look of dismay and surprise on her face! She hadn't seen that one coming and suddenly realised her weapon didn't work anymore, and she backed down and tried to laugh off the whole incident as a big joke. I decided then I wanted to leave and packed up all my belongings, but in the end did not have the finance to move. I was firmly stuck in the mud, in an impossible unhappy situation with no apparent way out.

Before the dust settled, she came home one evening and told me she had been fired from her job! *Wham!* Another clout alongside the head that mentally knocked me to the floor. Following on its heels she found out then that she didn't have a pension! Now we were destitute, and our only income now came from the small SA government pension I got which would not feed us for a week, let alone pay any rent! The lady had been in the same line of work for the last 25 years and had held managerial positions, but she was the only non-black left in the firm as it had now been Africanised. The truth is, they simply worked her out of her position using false accusations so they could fill her position with one of their own race. Apartheid in reverse. That's the way it is in South Africa!

The battle for survival

Now began the battle for survival! In this situation you soon learn that charity *does not* pay very well. It is fickle, and people take advantage of your situation offering you a little financial reward for doing something that makes them look good and benefits them more than yourself. We had to start accepting food parcels donated by the church going people. They believed they are doing good by giving to the poor and give themselves a pat on the back. Yet so often it was the cheap stuff they got from the supermarket, not the good stuff they would get for themselves. One-ply toilet paper instead of the strong two-ply they used. I am not ungrateful, it kept us alive. But it would only last us a few days and then it would be back to having one egg on one slice of bread for dinner, and that's all you had to eat for the day, apart from the bowl of bean soup we could get for free from the church soup kitchen in the morning, and that made you fart all day! We lived like this for a year. The founder of this church's religion had taught, 'Make as much money as you can. Save as much money as you can and *give away* as much money as you can.' He was big on giving to the poor, but in the end, he had to admit that his followers did not adhere to the last part of that teaching, and the poor were still poor! Nothing much has changed today, regardless of which religion is involved. Church going people still have short arms and long pockets where they can't reach the bottom, and that is contrary to what they are taught in church! I don't know how many times we would get a little money from somewhere and I would take the car down to the petrol station only to run out of petrol on the way.

We were deep into The Valley of the Shadow! Things got darker when the house came up for auction by the bank. We went to the auction which was held on the courthouse steps and took note of who bought the property. Afterwards we approached the new owner and explained our situation to him, asking if we could stay on in the flat in exchange for being caretakers of the property as it also had six two-bedroom flats on it making it an income property. The new owner agreed! We were elated, there was a little light at the end of the tunnel, and we could breathe a little easier.

But, the light at the end of the tunnel quickly turned into an express train bearing down on us at full speed. The deal fell through when the new owner couldn't pay the deposit. The sheriff of the court soon appeared at our door again with the 'good news' and told us the property would be auctioned off again in two months' time. Our hearts sank and our emotions were turned upside down again, but we waited out the time and again went to the next auction. This time however, the new owner was not so obliging and gave us one month to vacate the premises, or all our belongings would be dumped on the street! That was the month of November,

Jon Rhodie

and the pressure was on to find somewhere else to live. I appealed to everyone I knew, looking for a room, anything anyone could help us with, and found those who had assured us with promises of, 'If you need help, just call me', all faded into the fog that hung over The Valley of the Shadow. I was in the depths of despair and battling with depression. When would this end! How long could I continue before I just gave up? How long before my bleached bones joined those already littering the floor of The Valley of the Shadow?

We appealed to our church for help. They had a small flat at the back of the church that they rented out and it would fall vacant at the end of November. We spoke to the Rev' in charge, explained our circumstances, and offered our services as caretakers of the church and its grounds in exchange for the use of the flat. He sympathised with us and was sure the church would help us, but he would have to speak to the church committee first, the body of people that dealt with the spiritual and financial wellbeing of the church and its property, and they were due for their monthly meeting in a week's time. I felt at ease, feeling sure that the church where I had ministered at and been involved in for the last seven years would make the flat available to us, in the true spirit of Christian brotherhood. I mean, didn't the Good Book say, 'Help those in need, especially those of the household of faith'?

A week later the Rev' called us to his office and said, "I'm sorry, the committee had decided that they would rather rent out the flat again [to an outsider] *because the church needs the money!"* I was shocked! Devastated! You could have knocked me to the floor with a feather. Was there not one of the 12 strong committee who had the spiritual faith to believe for that money? The only other option open to us was an offer

13

by a widow lady of mixed race to share her two-bedroom flat with us in a mixed-race rundown housing project, and she had two small children. It's always the poor who are willing to help the poor. I could not see myself living there. Loads of snot-nosed children running up and down the staircase next to the flat all day playing and screaming their heads off! Men and women sitting outside your window on a wall in the evening smoking cannabis and drinking beer to all hours. The road was not even tarred, and the dust bellowed in through the windows. Weekends were one big party! The noise was often overwhelming and I'm sure I would have gone stark raving mad within a month and joined those sitting on the wall smoking funny tobacco! Laughing and giggling at all who walked past! I was in despair. I had nowhere left to turn! Somehow, I had to hang on to the hope that I would get through The Valley. How, I did not know!

Tension in in our marriage was at an all-time high. I was sleeping on the outer edge of the seam of the mattress as it was, and it was a ticking time bomb before the next major fight erupted. When it came it was not the usual screaming match, but quiet controlled anger which lasted for over an hour. We were sitting up in bed and I had spoken out against something she was doing which was wrong and which offended me. She had responded in the same old way by defending herself and laying all the blame on me. The sort of argument I just couldn't win! Then she opened the back door again, and this was the furthest thing on my mind at the time. But she tried reverse psychology this time, and suddenly out of nowhere said, "This time if **YOU** want to leave, I will not try and stop you!" not that she tried much the last time! Then she added, "And, **I** will sue you for divorce!" That of course would absolve her of all blame, as she could say I deserted her.

The gauntlet was thrown down. But by now I just didn't give a dam anymore and accepted the challenge as any Sag' would do. With the anger boiling in me I replied, "Fine, in that case, I'm leaving, and you can do your damnedest!" The decision was forced on me and it was time to get out of the situation. It was time to make the change. Maybe this was my ticket out of The Valley of the Shadow. There the fight ended abruptly, and I went and slept on the couch. Next morning, I got cardboard boxes and began to pack the remaining possessions I had left. I didn't know where the road would lead or how I would get there, but I had that firm resolve fixed in my mind fuelled by intense anger. I would find a way! If ever I needed unseen forces to come to my aid, it was now! But it was time for the centaur to trot of to a safe place.

The Good Samaritans

There was possibly only one person left that I could appeal to, and that was my lifelong friend David who lived far away down the coast. I did not want to burden him and his family with my problems, but he was the only one left! After that, there was no one else! In fear I picked up the phone and called him. He listened to my long tail of woe, and although he had empathy towards me, he said in fairness to his family he would need to discuss it with the rest of his family first. Next morning, he phoned me back and said, "My brother, we can't pay for you to come down, but if you can get here, we will give you a room to stay in, and help you in any way we can." I sat there and cried. Here was the Good Samaritan I needed. But I didn't have the faintest idea of how I would get down to his place. November had come and gone, and between me and my friend we searched for a way to get me down there. No trains went to their small town, and bus services were not prepared to take my ten boxes or my dog. Then, out of the blue a few days before Christmas, his daughter at random asked a group of women if they knew of anyone coming down from Durban who had a pickup truck. Then the miracle happened! One lady asked why, and she explained my situation. To which she replied, "My brother is coming down tomorrow towing a big boat. Your friend could put his boxes in that." She immediately phoned her brother and he readily agreed and said he would pick me up at eight o'clock in the morning. Unseen forces **HAD** come to my aid! This was the first in a line of miracles to take place.

It was as if a huge weight lifted off my shoulders, but there was that little nagging fear in the back of my mind that it would all disappear like mist in the morning. I spent a restless night half awake and prayed for the dawn. But the dawn did come, and at eight o'clock in the morning a big blue BMW pulled up outside my gate, towing a big white power boat. In short time I loaded all my boxes and cases into the boat and fastened the cover down. I said goodbye to my friends in the house and the driver and I climbed into the front seats. My little Foxy dog jumped up and sat on my lap. She loved a car ride and sat on my lap watching the road as we pulled off. I remember looking at that familiar street I had walked and driven down so many times, and it was like seeing it for the first, yet also the last time. I was on my way, and I knew I would not pass that way again!

Down to the T-junction at the end of the road. Left turn, right turn, and a few traffic lights later we took the on-ramp and joined the four-lane highway heading out of town. The big Beamer effortlessly ate up the miles and soon passed the coastal towns dotted along the coast. I sat in silence as we climbed up into the mountains and on to the long road through the rural areas which all seemed to flow past in a detached blur. I had driven this road many times and knew it well. I didn't speak much on the eight-hour journey, lost in my own thoughts. My little dog curled up on my lap and slept happily for the duration of the journey, totally unaware of the turmoil going on in my mind. There is a song that goes, 'Where are we going, I don't know. When will we get there I ain't certain? All that I know is I am on my way!' I had made the change but didn't have the faintest idea of what lay ahead. I was 69 years old with a grey beard. I had hardly any money and didn't have any prospects for the future. The one thing that was uppermost in my mind was that I could not just expect my mate David to support me and pay for my needs. I had to find a way to support myself, but what job opportunities do you have in a small town when you are 69? I was consumed with these thought that went round and round in my brain like a funfair carousel blearing out loud music, and where there was no way to get off. But the light at the end of the tunnel was real sunlight this time, and I felt I was beginning to emerge from The Valley of the Shadow.

The Law of Attraction

From somewhere in the storehouse of my subconscious mind there emerged the remembrance of a time some years back before I remarried, when I needed a miracle, and got one. The year was 2008. I had taken a fall and had torn the muscles in my right leg above the knee and around the hip. An extremely painful injury to the point I could not move without screaming in pain. I have broken bones before and had never screamed with pain, but this was intense pain like I had never experienced before. I landed up in hospital for two weeks before I could walk on crutches, and then spent another six weeks sitting at home with my leg on a stool before I could begin to put weight on it. Getting around was difficult and it was still some time before the muscles healed completely. At this time, if I needed to go shopping, I would have to walk on crutches for about a quarter of a mile to the bus stop. There was no bus shelter, so I would have to stand in the hot African sun for up to an hour before a bus came along. Then I would have to climb up three steep steps on crutches to board the bus, pay the driver and hope to make it to a seat before he took off down the road again. Most were considerate and waited until I found a seat, but a few times I had to play Tarzan the Ape Man swinging from the handrails along the roof! On the return journey I would be laden down with grocery bags and by the time I reached home again I was very sore and exhausted tired.

Somewhere around this time I discovered the Natural Law of Attraction. I didn't know it by that name then, but I read something somewhere and it referred to a passage in the Bible in Mark 11:24, where it says, *'Whatsoever things you desire, when you pray, **BELIEVE** that you **receive**, and you **shall** have them.'* A very simple concept that has been overlooked by the church because they don't understand it. Yet, it has always been there since the beginning of time! Here was Jesus teaching about Natural Law! So, it is not a religious thing. Jesus also taught about other Natural Laws such as the Law of Planting and Reaping as in the Parable of the Sower, which has also been around since the earth came into existence. What you sow, that shall you also reap! The Law of Attraction is like magnetism. If you take two magnets and hold them end on end one way, they attract powerfully to each other and connect. But, if you turn one the other way around, they will repel strongly against each other, and you will not be able to make them connect. The whole of the cosmos is ruled by the Law of Attraction and Repulsion. The earth has a natural magnetic field around it which controls our gravity and keeps our feet on the ground, and at the same time keeps the earth at the exact right distance in its orbit around the sun. Any closer and we would all burn up. Any further away and we would all freeze. So, there is nothing strange or creepy about the Natural Law of Attraction. It has just been misunderstood until now. There are plenty of books for sale explaining the subject.

Standing at the bus stop one day I decided that I needed my own transport. As my income was very limited, I decided that a scooter would be the least expensive form of transport, but, as I had no money to buy one, I decided to try Asking and Believing to get one. As this is a Natural Law you do not have to involve religion when using it. However, it can be found written into most major religions of the world, and as I am of the Christian persuasion, I chose to address my request to God as I know Him. So, I Asked for a scooter and began to believe that I would receive one. Faith and belief in the Bible mean exactly the same thing, they come from the same Greek word. But when exercising faith or belief one must build up that belief, and that is done by continually affirming what you believe as if it already exists! Persistence and determination are the key. So, every day, and as many times as I could think of it, I repeated the affirmation, "I believe I have got a scooter, and I WILL have one!" Blind faith! And you do not accept that it will turn out any other way!

This carried on every day for two months. If you give up and start thinking it's not working, it will not work! You have lost and have sown the seed in your life for future failure! Each day as many times as I could I repeated the affirmation using heart felt emotion and determination, and my expectation mounted until it became fact in my mind. I would have what I had asked for! The Law of Attraction is not a get rich scheme and you are not likely to win the Lotto either. Nor is it prosperity teaching. That to me is like a church pyramid scheme where only the pastors at the top clergy become rich and live in luxury. Mega churches have been built using it, and in the end, they fail and fall apart.

One Saturday morning I woke up and was thinking of what to do with myself that day, when a very strong thought entered my mind. It was so dominant that it startled me! It said, "Get up and go down to Jeff's Bikes, and choose yourself a scooter!" This was nuts! I didn't have any money to buy myself a scooter, but the urging was so strong that I didn't question it, and I got up and walked down to Jeff's Bikes on my crutches, which was a short distance from where I lived, and walked on to the showroom floor. After looking around a while at all the nice new shiny bikes and scooters for sale, I spotted a beautiful bronze coloured scooter standing in the second row with a price tag on it for SAR 10,000. I didn't have ten brass cents to rub together, but the urging was so strong that I went over to it and laid my hands on the saddle, and quietly asked, "Could I have this one please?" Then turned and walked out of the showroom and went home. Part of my backyard had an iron roof over it, under which was used to store all sorts of stuff, and as I passed this space, again I had the urging, "Well, if you are going to get a scooter, you need to clear a space to park it!" So, I did, right there and then! And for the next two weeks every time I walked past that empty space I said, "Thank you Lord for my scooter!" I got excited, and in my mind's eye I could see it standing there! I didn't know how, or when, but I just knew I had it! Anyone hearing me talk to an empty space would have thought I had lost my marbles, but to me it was now fact!

This is not an instant coffee type thing; it often has to percolate. It's like circumstances and people have to get into line first before what you Ask for, the unseen, becomes the seen, and comes into reality. All the dots have to line up. After two weeks my daughter suddenly came over from England on a surprise visit unannounced. I was very pleased to see her and one of the first things she said to me was, "Dad, I want to buy you a good second-hand motorbike for transport." In my mind I could see the new shining bronze scooter! 'Second-hand?' I thought to myself, 'Well, that's not my problem. I have Asked for a new scooter!' The next day we went round and looked at a few second-hand bikes and there was really nothing worth having. When we went back to my place, I was actually glad we hadn't found a second-hand bike! The next day, my daughter came to me at about mid-morning and said, "Dad, I have decided not to buy you a second-hand bike, instead I am going to buy you a NEW one." My spirit soared and hit the ceiling! She continued, "I have been round to some of the dealers in town and would like to take you with me to show you the type of bike and price range I have in mind. If there is a bike you like, I will get it for you." I was filled with excitement as we climbed into the car. It was really happening! I was going to get what I had Asked for! And where was the first dealership she took me to? – Just down the road to JEFF'S BIKES!!

My miracle scooter

My daughter walked with me on to the showroom floor and stopped in front of a scooter that was exactly the same make as the scooter I had chosen, just a little less fancy. Standing right next to it was the bronze scooter! I could hardly contain myself! Pointing to the price ticket she said, "This is the price range I have in mind, so take a look around and if there is something you like, it's yours." Without hesitation I pointed at the bronze scooter and said, "Could I have that one please?" She looked shocked and asked, "Are you sure? Don't you want to go round the other dealers and look at other scooters?" Hell's bones! I had never been more sure of anything in my life before!! "No." I assured her, "That's the one!" So, she sat down with the salesman and began the paperwork. Meanwhile I went and sat on the bronze scooter, laid my hands on the controls on the handlebars, and began to cry quietly. My daughter looked around and saw me crying and came over and asked what the matter was, and I told her the story of how just two weeks before I had laid my hands on the seat of that exact same scooter and asked God if I could have it! She was amazed and simply said, "Well there you are, that's God for you." The next day, once the scooter had been licenced and number plates put on, I went down and collected her from Jeff's Bikes, and drove her home and parked her in the space I had cleared for her! What I had Asked for, and repeated as affirmations, and visualised, had now become reality!

The three goals

I didn't use the Law of Attraction again for three years, it got stored away in my subconscious half-forgotten until that day it came to my remembrance on that trip going away from Durban. I felt now was the time to use it again. Gradually a firm resolve began to form in my mind, and I established three affirmations, or goals, in my mind. These are –

(1) *I WILL have my own house to live in!*
(2) *I WILL have a good salary to live on!* and
(3) *I WILL have a good vehicle to drive!*

I began to repeat these three affirmations over and over quietly to myself until they became fixed in my mind. They would be the star to guide me during the next few months. I didn't have the faintest idea how I would achieve these three goals, they almost seemed impossible, but *fortune favours the brave, and to the victor the spoils!* Hours later we arrived at our destination and my mate David was waiting for me at the pick-up point. To this day I cannot not remember the name of the owner of the BMW as my mind was in turmoil during the trip and we talked very little. But I am eternally grateful to him for coming to my aid.

Chapter 2

We loaded my goods and shackles on to the back of my mate David's Land Rover, said our goodbyes to the BMW driver and were soon on the rough dirt road heading out to his farm. I felt happy and more at ease than I had felt for a long time, but my emotions were still in turmoil, and I felt drained of any feelings. I had arrived at my destination but still didn't know how things were going to work out or what I was going to do from there on. However, the first objective had been reached and tomorrow would have to take care of itself. At the farm, the whole family turned out to greet me, and a very warm welcome it was indeed, with hugs and kisses and handshakes all round. We loaded my boxes into the garage, and I was shown to the room I always occupied whenever I came to visit. Everything about the house felt so permanent and stable, like nothing had changed since I was there last. I felt at peace and safe but still unsure about the future. David had taken one look at me and taken the rest of the family aside. "Just leave that boy alone," he had said to them. "He is hurting and needs time to get his head together again."

And so they did, they gave me all the time I needed. They bound up my emotional wounds with love, kindness and empathy, and left me to myself to go for long walks along the farm roads and let my spirit get quiet. I would seek solitude at the bottom of the garden and sit quietly under a big shady Lucky Bean tree. It is a big wide knobbly tree that gets a beautiful red flower in summer, which turn into a long bean like pod filled with little red bean seeds. When dry, the pod would burst and scatter the seed all around. You could pick up a handful just sitting under the tree. Sitting there just feeling the sun shining down on me was like coming out of the dark muddy Valley of the Shadow, on to the sunlit plains of the Serengeti Game Reserve in Tanzania. It stretches out for as far as the eye can see and is covered in knee-high grass with tall umbrella shaped trees dotted across the landscape. Rivers run through it filled with cool clear water to refresh my raging thirst, and it is covered with a multitude of wildlife of every description. Paradise! Christmas came and went in a bit of a blur. Other people came over on Christmas Day and we had a fine meal, but I can't remember their faces. Back in Durban we would have been lucky to have been able to have a chicken for lunch, so I was extremely grateful for a lovely meal.

It took about six weeks for my head and my thoughts to clear while I was sitting under the Lucky Bean tree. I began to focus on how I was going to support myself in the future. Every day I continued repeating the three affirmations I had made and now my subconscious mind began to work on how to achieve them. I kept on saying the three affirmations I had worked out on the way down. I repeated them to myself with fierce determination. *'I WILL have my own house to live in! I WILL have a good salary to live on! And I WILL have a good vehicle to drive!'* I don't know how this works, but I have used affirmations before with great success, as in the case with the scooter. You need to put them down on paper. What you continually feed into your mind with firm determination becomes fact, and somehow the unseen forces bring it into reality.

I spent a day in town going from firm to firm and shop to shop asking for employment but came up empty handed, which is much of what I expected. Nobody wants you when you are 69. So, I sat down under the Lucky Bean tree and thought about what I had to offer, what did I have to work with? In life, you have three choices, *Improvise*, *Adapt or Overcome*. I was healthy, I have had military and security experience. I grew up on a farm and have done farming, so can handle labour, and I owned my own guns. Herein was a niche I could fit into. Farm invasions are common in South Africa, and many farmers have been murdered and their guns, household property and vehicles stolen by the indigenous. Many farmers are afraid to leave their farms unattended or go on holiday, because their place will be stripped bare in their absence. Just like people do housesitting in the cities, I decided to try farm-sitting, and look after people's farms for them while they were away. To this end I made up an advert, listing what I could offer, and went back into town with a hundred flyers and stuck them up in every shop window and supermarket noticeboard I could find. I then found that for a small fee, the post office would put them into post boxes for me, so I put another 200 in there and sat back and waited. I wasn't sure if this would work but had to try.

To my huge relief the first call came in within days of me putting out the flyers. A smallholding farm where a man lived alone, and he had to go into hospital for two weeks. And so began an incredible journey. Up to this point everything in Durban had been going downhill like it was going out of season. Now everything turned around, and like the advert for a well know brand of vehicle, everything kept going right! I was bold in the price I charged for my services and was a little worried about this in the beginning, but soon found my clients did not consider this unreasonable and were willing to pay my price.

There was not much to do on this smallholding. He had a few pigs which I didn't have to feed, thank goodness, as the next-door neighbour saw to that. Otherwise, there were chickens to take care of and two dogs to feed. A cleaner came in each day to take care of the house, but she often turned up drunk or not at all. I went for long walks with the dogs and soon learned to stick to the roads because the bush areas were full of little red ticks about the size of a pinhead called pepper ticks, for good reason, as their bite burned like fire! The only time I went walking in the grass I came back with my legs covered in them from the knees down and had to carefully de-tick myself and the dogs as they have a fiery bite and can give you tick bite fever, which is very unpleasant. Time dragged by and when the farmer came home, he asked me to stay on for another week while he regained his strength. This farm was about two hours' drive from my mate's place, and for the return journey it was arranged for me to get a ride in a big 18-wheeler truck and trailer. This was different, I had never been in one before, sitting up high watching small cars go by on the road almost beneath you.

I felt good! My endeavour had borne fruit and I now had a little money in my pocket. I could pay my way again, and not feel like I was dependant on my mate's generosity. Memories of having to live on charity still haunted me. I spent time sitting under the Lucky Bean tree again, feeling free, but anxiously waiting for my phone to ring with the next job offer. I had to wait for about a month before the call came, and this job was a real beauty. Everything kept going right!

Just down the road from David's place is a wildlife ranch. The manager was going on holiday for six weeks and at the last minute the man who was going to look after the place had to pull out. Luckily, they spotted my flyer in town and gave me the job. Lucky for me! This was right up my ally as I was raised in the bush and love all things wild, and I am a wildlife artist. What better could I wish for!

The ranch had a deep wide lush green valley running through it. It was geared for tourism, and a small river ran through it. The homestead was situated halfway up the hill and was only accessible by a rough dirt road which was the only way in or out. For security reasons this was ideal. I might just as well have been in the Serengeti! There was an abundance of game of every description. Zebra came to shelter from the hot sun under the lean-to that served as a parking garage, right outside the kitchen door. Impala buck and warthogs grazed around the house just outside the garden fence. Giraffe and wildebeest antelope came to drink at the water hole a hundred yards from the house in the evening. I had to remind myself that these were wild animals and needed to be treated as such. This was not a zoo! I was as happy as a pig in – um – mud! The house itself was a rustic old tin roof farmhouse with loads of charm, and as quiet as a church on Mondays. Now, the vehicle I had to use was something else! An old beat up green V8 Land Rover fitted out with game viewing seats on the back. It had a suspect gearbox that wouldn't engage first gear and was difficult to get into reverse or four-wheel drive. As the roads were so steep or windy you drove everywhere in second gear from the start! The petrol tank? Well, that was a 20-litre plastic drum tied down in the back of the vehicle, with a plastic pipe sticking out of it to feed the carburettor! But it worked! I had lots of fun driving that thing and it could still go anywhere, in second gear of course! Although I did nearly get stuck down a ravine once when I couldn't find reverse gear or get the stupid thing into 4x4! I named it the Antichrist!

I had a few more chores to do here. There was a backpackers camp down by the river that had to be kept clean. Oil lamps had to be filled up and firewood hauled in. The camp was very basic but comfortable and designed to give the tourists the bush experience. They would come up the river by canoes as far as they could go, then had an hour's hike on foot to the camp through the bush walking among the wildlife. Great fun was had by all. Then I had to collect the fence repair team each morning from up the other side of the valley, take them to where they needed to go along roads that were a challenge to my 4x4 driving skills, and collect them again in the afternoon. In the time in between I could just sit and watch the wildlife or work on a painting of a lion's head and shoulders I was doing for the manager and his wife when they got back. My little dog was fascinated by the game, especially the giraffe with their long necks. She had never seen anything like them before! We once sat for an hour in the Land Rover surrounded by a dozen giraffe that grazed from the tops of the trees a few yards from us while my dog stared up at them. The giraffe were unconcerned by our presence and looked down on my little dog with bemused interest. The African name for them is, 'Taller than the trees.'

A person's 70th birthday is a huge milestone in their life, you have reached three score and ten years of age. I celebrated my 70th with my extended family from the farm in the valley of the ranch at a picnic spot where we had a lovely BBQ. Big shady trees shielded us from the hot November sun. The smell of wood smoke with meat cooking over the coals and all sorts of wildlife grazing a short distance away, made for a very memorable day. As a kid I had never had many birthday parties as I was always away at boarding school, so this one was special!

All to soon the six weeks were up and the manager and his wife returned from their holiday. They were thrilled with the painting of the lion and immediately hung it on their wall. Sadly, I said my goodbye's and left the ranch. It was a beautiful experience and a far cry from squatting penniless in a small flat without lights and water, and a hostile wife for company! How life had changed in the year since I made the change.

As my second wife had not filed for divorce as she had threatened, I proceeded to initiate the proceedings. I got a DIY kit from the local bookshop as I couldn't afford an attorney and went to the local legal aid office to ask them to help me fill it in and get the proceedings started. The lady listened to my story and then said that since I was unemployed and entitled to legal aid, would I like them to do it all for me? Far out! That would save me a lot of hassle and a lot of money. The long and the short of it is that one year later I got my divorce, free of charge! Now here is a strange coincidence. The divorce came through exactly on the same date as I got married on! Was this coincidence? Or was it an omen, or a sign, that this marriage should not have taken place in the first place, because Scorpio and Sagittarius are a bad mix? I don't know, but it was the end of a chapter and I never looked back. It is easy to say, 'You must forgive', and I did forgive, but it is not so easy to forget the hard, unpleasant times one goes through. Only time will erase the scars that are left behind. But I was free again!

I had now saved up enough money to buy myself a small 125cc street motorbike. Not a good idea for rough dirt roads, but it was all I could get hold of at the time. Now I was independent and didn't have to inconvenience my mate to transport me here and there. It had been a long time since I could afford to get my own transport and I enjoyed getting out and about on it, regardless of the fact that the dirt roads nearly rattled my brains to pieces inside my helmet! But! The wheel of life was turning, and it was going up!

I had to play the waiting game for a while till I got the call for my next job. This was on a resort farm that did hiking and bike riding trails. They had a number of nice, thatched self-service chalets, and an area out in the bush with big family sized tents for the camping enthusiasts. It was the off season so there weren't any visitors around, and the owner had to go away on business for a month. I had the guest cottage to stay in which was very comfortable. They had two big dogs who just wanted to bite holes in my little dog, but this was not too much of a problem as his wife stayed behind at home and controlled the dogs, so my job was mainly security to protect her while her husband was away. When she heard I was an artist she expressed her interest in painting but didn't know how to go about it. So, I agreed to teach her a bit and spent time doing a picture with her using acrylic paint. I must admit her painting turned out very well. She had the talent, and she was bitten by the painting bug and was keen to carry on painting in the future. For the rest of the month, I spent a lazy time relaxing or walking their hiking trails which ran through some beautiful scenery.

After that job I went through a period of drought where no jobs came in for over two months, and I was getting worried as money was beginning to run low. Then sitting under the Lucky Bean tree one day contemplating my future, I felt the urge to go to another small coastal town about 30 miles down the coast and put up some of my flyers on the notice board of their local supermarket. I have learned to listen to these inner urgings, so the next day I hoped on my bike and headed for the town. The wind was very strong that day and blowing head on, which made riding the bike very difficult, and at one stage I considered turning back because the wind was so strong, but I decided to press on. I got to the town which is more of a holiday destination but there are many big farms in the area and a few wildlife resorts. The supermarket was quite big and supplied the whole area, so I considered it a good place to advertise my services. I put the flyers up on the noticeboard and got on the bike and made the return journey, going flat out with the wind behind me pushing me all the way. Now the outcome was in the lap of the gods, and I sat down to wait.

The wildlife ranch

I was really getting quite worried. It is so easy for doubt to creep in when nothing seems to be happening, and I had to continually guard against this. I started asking my God to bless me according to **His WORD,** good measure, pressed down, shaken together, and running over! Exceedingly abundantly above that which I thought or asked! The Law of Attraction states that if you *believe* you receive, you *shall* have it! It is not about *who* you Ask. Believing that you shall receive is the Key! That is why a Buddhist can go up a mountain to a shrine and Ask his god, and he will receive his miracle! Because HE believes! Or someone can Ask Mother Mary for a miracle, and they will get it! It is more like sending your request out into the cosmos, where it is received and passed on to the storehouse of riches in glory, and the answer is returned to you. Why does this happen? It is the power of belief that brings the answer. It's Natural Law, and we all have the ability to believe! When something bad happens to a person we often hear them say, "I just *knew* that was going to happen!" They believed it, and they received it. The Law of Attraction works both ways. Bad things happen because of wrong thinking, and thoughts become experiences. Your life can become transformed by the renewing of your mind, which is the origin of your thoughts! Change your *thinking* from bad to good and you will change your life and circumstances. If you sit around worrying that something bad is going to happen to you, that is what you will attract to yourself! The Attitude of Gratitude can make a tremendous difference in your life. Make a practice of writing down on paper all the things that you are grateful for going back to childhood. Are you grateful that you have a roof over your head and food to eat? Millions in the world today are not so fortunate! You will attract to yourself more of all the things you are grateful for today.

I didn't have to wait long. It was a Saturday morning a few days later when my phone rang. To my surprise, the voice on the other end was American! Not many of them in South Africa! The man introduced himself and explained he owned a wildlife ranch not far from the coastal town where I had just put up my adverts. I was thinking, 'Oh good! Another job on a wildlife ranch!' He said he had seen my advert at the local supermarket, and it looked like I was the type of man he was looking for. This sounded promising and he asked me a few questions as we chatted. Then I began to realise he was talking about a ***permanent*** position! As the manager of his wildlife ranch! Not just looking after the place for a while! I was amazed and excited. I gave him the name of the owner of the first wildlife ranch where I had spent six weeks as a reference, and he said he would set up a time sometime next week where we could meet and have an interview, and we ended the call. Excitement ran through my veins like ice cold liquid fire! Here I was at the age of 70, being offered the chance of becoming the manager of a wildlife ranch! A far cry from squatting in an abandoned house with no electricity and living on charity in Durban, that is for sure! When I shared the news with David and the rest of the family they were amazed and shared my excitement! I couldn't wait for next week to have the interview!

I didn't have to wait for next week! He phoned me back the very next day on Sunday morning and asked if I could come out to the ranch immediately for an interview! My mate told me to take a Land Rover and I set off like a shot. The American met me at the remote-controlled gate to the ranch, where I left my Land Rover and climbed into his new top of the range V8 Land Rover. His wife was with him, a very lovely lady, and I liked them both instantly. They were down to earth, very nice people. We went down to the main house along a well-kept dirt road. There were herds of impala buck everywhere, and we passed some giraffe next to the road who peered down at us from above the trees with enquiring interest. His house was a beautiful open-plan place with big glass doors which opened out on to a wide wooden deck which ran around the front of the house. The lounge was spacious and nicely furnished with a chandelier hanging from the ceiling, yet not overdone. There was plenty of light coming in from the large windows that faced out on to the deck. From the deck the terrain dropped down steeply some distance to the floor of the wide valley below, giving a spectacular view of the flat valley floor spreading out on either side, flanked by green hills which rose up in a V shape on either side and disappeared off into the distance. He had a round swimming pool on the edge of the deck which looked directly down the steep slope into the valley. A river ran through it, snaking in from the right and meandering and twisting till it disappeared far into the distance. We sat at the counter by the kitchen which had black marble counter tops all round and had coffee. I remember him asking me if I wanted cream with my coffee and had to think for a second before realising, he meant milk. After coffee, with cream, he took me on a tour of the ranch in his Land Rover. The ranch was quite big, about a thousand acres, and it took us some time to go round it. It was well stocked with all sorts of buck of all shapes and sizes, including big eland and kudu, and warthogs by the hundred. In one paddock there was a small heard of beautiful black sable antelope. Very valuable animals. The bull had been imported from Tanzania. He was a magnificent animal in his prime, standing proud and tall with beautiful long curved horns arching over his back. He also had a herd of about 50 cape buffalo. In hunting circles, they are known as the black death because they are so dangerous, and many stories abound of hunters being killed by buffalo. Warthogs on the other hand are comical as they run away from you, all in a line with their tails pointing straight up in the air like radio antennas. He showed me the two bomas used to capture buffalo when needed. Large paddocks which you could herd the buffalo into. Not as easy as it sounds, but I'll tell you more about that later.

After the tour he took me back to the gate and told me he would have to make a decision and would contact me again sometime during the next week. I was very impressed with the ranch and drove home feeling very excited. I had been shown the manager's house which was a two-bedroom bungalow with black marble kitchen counters and bath surround. The lounge was quite large with big glass windows that looked out on to a wide wooden deck that ran around the front of the bungalow and looked down into the valley. There was a chandelier hanging from the ceiling in the lounge and a small wood-burning stove standing in the corner for cold winters nights. The main bedroom had a wall of glass across the front of it, so you could lay in bed and look out across the valley. The nearest neighbours were miles away, so you didn't even have to close the curtains at night. Double glass doors opened out on to the wooden deck that ran around the front of the house and gave you spectacular views of the river and the valley below. It was a lovely quiet peaceful place. Chandeliers in the African bush was a little unusual, but what the heck! The next morning, Monday morning, my phone rang early in the morning and the American voice on the other end said, "Congratulations! You have got the job! When can you start?" Wow man! This was far out! I excitedly said I would start on Wednesday. That would give me enough time to pack my gear. It was like the door of opportunity had been opened, and all the dots lined up. I had been shoved inside, and the door slammed shut behind me before I could think! Phone call on Saturday, interview on Sunday, got the job on Monday, and start the job on Wednesday! Awesome! A true miracle! On Wednesday I moved out to the ranch and realised instantly that all three of my goals had become reality! I had my own house to live in. I had a salary that was well above average. And I had a big Land Cruiser pickup truck with huge wide tyres and a big powerful 4.2 litre engine in it as the vehicle I was to use! I had never driven such a powerful vehicle before! I was amazed, as were my mate's family. It just didn't get any better than that! Exceedingly, abundantly, above all that which I had thought or asked. The Law of Attraction works! All three of the things I had asked for on the way down from Durban came into reality the minute I stepped on to that ranch! I also had peace and tranquillity and was surrounded by loads of wildlife. I had made the move from Durban. I had set the three goals and written down the affirmations, which I had held powerfully in my mind as if I already had them. Suddenly, the miracle had happened! My life had gone from an unhappy anxiety filled poverty situation to that of peace, joy and abundant living! The Law of Attraction works! You just need to put in the time and effort!

Chapter 3

Over the next two weeks I settled into the work routine of the ranch and got to know the layout of the place. I only had three African labourers and I would sit with them in the morning, have coffee with them and plan out what work needed to be done that day. I had never really seen wild cape buffalo close up before and was told we put out food for them each day at the bottom boma. This was a type of hay called lucerne which is sweet tasting, and which supplemented their natural diet. This was placed inside the boma at 3 pm each day to entice them to enter and feed there, with the intention of being able to close the sliding gate and capture them inside when we needed to medicate them or capture some for sale. The boss had been trying for two months to capture the heard so they could be medicated, but buffalo, being cleaver animals, had given them the slip each time they tried. One afternoon I took the pickup and drove down to the boma around 3 pm to look at the Buffalo, to find them milling around outside the gate and beginning to go inside to feed. I stopped a little distance away from them and we eyeballed each other for a while. Buffalo will look at you with their heads raised, sort of down the end of their noses, if they feel threatened. Any move on your part could invoke a charge. If you are on foot then you start praying, 'Please God, get me up a tree, fast!'

As the pickup posed no threat to them, heads soon dropped, and their attention turned to the food inside and they began to leisurely stroll into the boma to feed. Slowly I inched the truck around to the right and used it to herd them like cattle into the boma. Some of them realised what I was up to and broke away and ran back into the bush, but I got a good number of them inside and was able to drive up to the gate, hop out the vehicle and slide the gate closed! Quite easily done, and I counted 35 of them inside the boma. The high fence around the boma is lined with black plastic sheeting so the animals inside cannot see out, this makes them think it is a solid wall and keeps them calm. Feeling very pleased with myself I drove back to the main house and casually said to the boss, "Oh – I have just captured 35 buffalo in the bottom boma." He looked at me in disbelief with one eyebrow raised. "You have just done – what!?" he enquired. So, I repeated myself again sort of matter of fact, and we immediately jumped into the pickup and headed for the boma. Shure enough, there were 35 buffalo inside it. The boss was impressed, he had been trying for two months to capture the buffalo, and I, by pure luck, had captured 35 of them on my first encounter! This also included the dominant male bull called Caesar, and his younger second in command sidekick who we needed to medicate as they both had mange. So began my love affair with the cape buffalo, and there were a few more adventures to come.

Activity on the ranch now kicked up a pace. The wildlife vet was contacted and booked to come out the next day, and ten casual African labours were organised to help with the buffalo. Most of these men had never even seen a wild buffalo in their life before, let alone handled one, so it was an adventure for them. Next day we all moved down to the boma with the vet, where the boss pointed out the animals that needed medicating and the vet set about darting them with a dart gun to anesthetise them, and soon we had about eight big buffalo asleep on the ground. Now we had to move fast, and we let the rest of the herd out of the gate. The job of the casual labour was to hold the head of the buffalo upright so they could breathe, otherwise they would suffocate. It was quite awesome to see the big bull Caesar, with all his brute strength asleep on the ground with his massive head being supported by a young African man, whom he could have easily killed with one swipe of his horns had he been awake. I laid my hand on his back and was surprised at how hot his hide felt. The men happily posed for photographs with big smiles on their faces. This was a picture that would gain them great prestige back at their home.

With all the medicating done the vet began to administer the antidote and woke them up one by one and we let them out the boma. All except Caesar, whom the boss wanted to keep in the boma for a few days for observation, he was woken up last. The big bull got up groggily to his feet and looked around taking in the scene for a few moments before he realised, he was alone in the boma! His whole darn herd had vanished! All his cows were gone! And what's more they were probably with that upstart of a young bull who was his sidekick! This was definitely not acceptable to him, and he took off at a gallop, an awesome ton of wild angry beef looking for a way out, and there was none! He looked like he had a massive bull-sized buffalo hangover. Two rounds of rampaging around the boma and he used those massive horns with its wide solid horny helmet shaped boss about 25 cm thick, to smash into a fencepost as thick as a man's thigh, and smashed it in half like matchwood, but the fence held! After butting a few more fenceposts he turned his attention to the holding pens where everyone was standing on top and charged hitting the steel sliding gate of one with ferocious power, bending the frame and getting it partially open before charging off down to the bottom of the boma trying to find another way out, but found none, which made him even more angry. He was an awesome frightening sight to behold!

The boss asked me if I could go into the boma with the truck and try and push the gate closed using the bull-bars on the front of the vehicle. I complied and drove into the boma and tried to push the gate closed. We didn't want him getting into the holding pen and causing havoc inside there. I felt quite safe as I was inside the vehicle and worked at trying to close the gate. Then, in the passenger side rear mirror I saw Caesar storming up behind the truck at full gallop, an awesome but terrifying sight of impending trouble. Big hooves pounded the dirt sending up clouds of dust, and I could hear him snorting loudly, but I was safe inside the vehicle. I felt the massive impact as he slammed into the steel bumper at the back of the vehicle and hooked a horn under it, shaking the vehicle and tossing it up and down a few times, lifting the rear wheel right off the ground effortlessly like a child playing with a toy. To say this was alarming to me is an understatement, and I thought I would have to go home and change my underpants! For a moment a huge drunken bloodshot buffalo's eye glared at me through the passenger side window before he smashed his horn into the left front fender, redesigning it completely and leaving the front bumper hanging on the ground, before galloping off down to the bottom of the boma. Raw, mad, wild power! Calls came from the top of the holding pens for me to get the hell out of there, and I wasted no time in doing so, and they just managed to get the sliding gate closed behind me as I exited the boma before Caesar came to a screeching halt in front of it snorting and puffing and stamping his hooves like a huge black wild demon. Wheeling round he charged at a part of the fence where the ground sloped down a drop of about six feet and took off at the top of the rise through the air and smashed into the fence below with the full one ton of his weight. The charge snapped off three thick fenceposts and flattened the fence, and Caesar was over it and out and off into the bush to find his herd. God help that young bull if he found he had been messing with any of his cows while he was away! And that was my baptism by fire into wildlife ranching! Or should I say, baptism by buffalo! I had a very healthy respect for the cape buffalo after that and regarded them with both cautious fear, and fondness.

The Good Life

The three goals I had set for myself on that long trip down from Durban had now been miraculously achieved, and I would not have to use the Law of Attraction again for some time. I had gone from thoughts held in my mind, the unseen, to the seen, or reality. Thoughts held strongly in the mind become things. On the ranch I settled into a life of ease and happiness in surroundings that were totally suited to my lifestyle. After the heat of the day, I would sit on the deck in the cool of late afternoon and watch giraffe walking down the hill to the valley below. And when darkness fell the sky above my head would be filled with trillions of stars, splashed out in all the glory of the milky way across the universe from horizon to horizon. The good salary that I received could be used solely for my own personal needs. I did not have to pay for rent or fuel or electricity, so my purse began to fatten. In my time on the ranch, I saved more than I had ever been able to save in my entire working career, and I was in the best job that I had ever had. Life was indeed very good, and I was exceedingly grateful for what I had. The memories of what I had endured before in poverty slowly faded into the background.

The boss and his lovely wife spent long periods away from the ranch, going on road trips to wilderness areas in surrounding African countries. Soon they left for Zambia for a few months, and I was left solely in charge of running the ranch. He also left me his 30.06 calibre hunting rifle, so I could take down a hog, as he called them (warthog) now and again for meat for the labourers. This is where my little dog came into her own. When I shot the first warthog, she jumped off the vehicle and ran after it like a hunting dog. This surprised me but there was nothing to fear as it was a clean shot and the warthog was down, but she worried it for a moment anyway until I called her off. This became the norm whenever I went hunting. She had never been trained to do this and it was pure instinct.

I watched the seasons change and the rains come and go. Early spring saw an explosion of new birth on the ranch. Little Bambi impalas with their long slender forever legs everywhere by the dozen. Baby zebras, kudu, sable, buffalo and giraffe appeared all over the place. So did the presence of jackals, to whom a baby buck was a very tasty meal, and the night-time became alive as they called to each other in the distance. But that is the law of the bush in Africa. I soon found there was an area of grass that was infested with ticks and lost several baby zebras to distemper. For me that was heart-breaking. I would have liked to have burned the grass in the area to kill the ticks but was not allowed to do so. But in all I was happier than I had been for a long – long time. I was living a dream! This, for me, was abundant living! I had a fantastic job. A lovely house to live in with a view to die for. A very good salary, and a big powerful 4x4 vehicle to ride around in!

Buffalo capture

When the boss got back, he got a sales order for five buffalo from another wildlife park. One cow with her calf, a spiker as they were called, with four-inch-long horns, and three young bulls of about five years old. The buffalo, who are clever animals, had changed their feeding time in the boma from 3 pm to 10 pm at night. I monitored the boma for a while using motion senser camaras to determine their movements. I then got two of my men to volunteer to spend the night in the hay storage shed next to the gate, and when it was safe to do so, one man sprinted over and closed the gate at about eleven o'clock, trapping a good number of buffalo inside.

Now the fun was on again! The vet was contacted to come out and dart the animals, and I called for the ten casuals to be picked up the next day. In fact, the enthusiasm was so great that when I went to pick them up from town, it wasn't until I got back to the ranch that I discovered I had 15 men on the back of the Land Cruiser, all keen to become wild buffalo wranglers! Not a problem, as we needed them all that day. The buffalo we needed were selected and anaesthetised using a dart gun, and Caesar and the rest of his herd were let out of the boma. Didn't want him running around the boma causing havoc again! No-sir-ree! One drugged up stoned young bull fell over into the water trough before he passed out and had to be rescued quickly and physically lifted out of it. We had to work quickly now and one by one the buffalo were manhandled by the men on to a sledge and towed up the slope by our 4x4 farm buggy to the holding pens amid much shouting and jubilation by the men, where they were again manhandled into the holding pens and given the wakeup antidote. It takes a lot of manpower to manoeuvre the weight of a sleeping one-ton buffalo, and the labourers were happy to pose for pictures with big, excited smiles on their faces. It was heavy work and afterwards the men posed for a few group photographs, and I was able to take them back to town and give them their well-earned wages. They had stories to tell their friends that night. They were wild buffalo wranglers!

The vet had examined the buffalo when they were knocked out and had given them a clean bill of health. Now we had to wait for the certificates to be issued by the state vet and the permits obtained to transport them to their new destination, and this would take some weeks. So, in the meantime they were kept in the holding pens and fed on lucerne hay each day. It was now near Christmas, and the boss went away on another road trip. My three permanent staff took their annual two weeks leave over Christmas and I was left alone on the ranch, which meant the daily feeding of the buffalo was left to me.

The holding pens were a solid log construction, with the logs planted vertically into the ground to a hight of about seven feet. The only other openings were the sliding gate and a square hole cut into the one wall which had a feeding trough on the inside which was surrounded by a steel grid of bars to protect the person putting in the feed from the buffalo on the inside. At first the buffalo stood a few meters away from the feed box as I loaded it with lucerne. I would speak quietly to them as I loaded the lucerne and over a few days they came to recognise I was the hand that fed them, and I was not a threat to them. Soon they were standing close up next to the feed box as I loaded it and began to eat before I had finished. On an impulse I picked up a handful of lucerne and extended my arm through the bars and offered it to the cow. She was suspicious at first then took a step closer and sniffed at my peace offering, then to my delight and surprise she took it from my hand and ate it! It was a magical moment! I tried again and offered her another handful, and she ate that too! Something very special happens when you gain that trust with a wild animal, especially with a dangerous wild cape buffalo! It is a mutual trust and friendship that is awesome, but I would not dare to venture in beyond those bars. My safety would not be guaranteed! I tried the same thing with the young bulls next door, but they would not take the feed from my hand, instead the one young bull sniffed my hand, then licked it a few times with his big rough tongue. Another magical moment, and I went home feeling elated! Every day after that the cow would take the feed from my hand, and the young bull would lick my hand. I felt a sense of loss when the trucks finally arrived, and they were loaded on them and taken away to their new home.

I was living in my own little paradise, far removed from the unpleasant times that had been my lot just over two years ago. But as often happens, even in paradise, there is someone who for reasons unknown decides to disturb your peace. My thorn in the flesh turned out to be a man who could have helped me a lot because of his knowledge of wildlife, but he chose not to do so. Instead, when the boss was away, he on two occasions emailed him and painted me in a dark light. This was accompanied by photos of my supposed neglect, like an empty water trough (that was not being used at that time). The truth is that the pump that was used to fill it was broken, and I could only get it fixed in a few days' time! I confronted him and we had words and he backed off, emphatically saying he was not after my job, but I didn't believe that. I was angry, but one of my staff, a Zulu man, said to me, "Don't worry about him! One day the baboon will miss the branch!" I laughed heartily and thought, 'Yes, *what you sow, that shall you also reap!*' It's another Natural Law as old as time, and you always reap more that you sow!

This was soon forgotten when my 71st birthday rolled around and I was able to spend the day with my friends, my extended family, on the ranch, where we had a good BBQ on the deck of my house overlooking the beauty of the valley. This was one of the few times in my life where I could splash out and have a really good party. No booze included as none of us drink, but just good food and good company. What more could a man wish for? In the afternoon we all climbed on to the Land Cruiser and I took them on a game drive all around the ranch. We were lucky enough to see the heard of buffalo grazing out in the open and get up close to the Sable antelope, the big bull posing proudly for photographs. A good day was had by all.

Some weeks later I unexpectedly fell ill and came down with a severe dose of bronchitis which laid me low for about two weeks. It was about all I could do to drag myself to the morning meeting with my staff and plan the work for the day. Then I would go back to bed, take meds, and lay there for the rest of the day feeling like death warmed up. As I recovered, I began to think, what would happen if, suddenly at my age, I couldn't work anymore? This was not negative thinking; it was time to consider my future. If for some reason due to illness or an accident I found myself in this position, how would I survive? The thought of landing up on the streets with no support and only a small government pension to live on certainly did not appeal to me. As much as I hated the idea of leaving the ranch, perhaps it was time to think of making a change. I Asked the Lord the question and committed it to the Law of Attraction to come up with the answer, and soon the answer came back. It was time to move again.

The Buffalo Fight Club

The boss and his wife were away on one of their road trips, and as I considered my options, the staff come to me all excited the next day and urged me to come quickly and bring my camera. Two buffalo were fighting in a clearing where we were feeding them, and they appeared to have their horns locked and couldn't get loose! Rushing to the clearing I found two buffalo cows locked in mortal combat pushing, shoving, bellowing, whirling round and round and raising clouds of dust. They looked exhausted and had obviously been going at it for hours. Then I noticed that they didn't just have their horns locked, they in fact had managed to get their horns locked around each other's necks! An impossible situation to get out of! How they managed that, I don't know, because the space between their curved horns at the top was only about 15 cm, or six and a half inches wide, and a buffalo's neck is very thick. To get free one would have to pull its head downwards to free its horn from under the others neck, but in doing that the horn of the other buffalo would choke it, while its own horn would press down on the top of its adversary's neck against its helmet of horns, so preventing it from getting free, and vice-versa.

Big game hunters of old have told stories of occasionally finding the skeletons of game such as buffalo and kudu in the bush with their horns locked in a death struggle. They must have died a grim death of starvation or thirst, or perhaps been attacked by predators as the lay there defenceless. There was only one way to get them free, and that was to cut a horn off each of them. But no self-respecting wild cape buffalo would stand there calmly while a human sawed off its horn with a hand saw! I certainty would not volunteer for the job either. Hell hath no fury like an angry and contentious buffalo cow! I called in a local wildlife vet who was experienced in untangling buffalo, and he came out to the ranch as quickly as he could to assess the situation. He said in all his years of experience he had never seen two buffalo so locked up like this. This was a unique situation very rarely, if ever, witnessed by humans. The only answer was to anesthetise both by darting them, then cut the horns.

The vet got to work and darted both of them, and in minutes they were asleep on the ground. We rushed into the tangle of thick bush and vines where they had fallen with bow saws and got ready to cut the first horn, but then the vet stopped us. First, he touched the open eyeball of one buffalo with his finger, and then did the same to the other buffalo, and they did not blink! They were both dead! When they went down in their weakened state, they had strangled each other to death in less than two minutes. All we could do was stand there and look down at a million SA rands worth of dead buffalo laying at our feet. For me it was a very sad moment as these two beautiful beasts met an untimely and unfortunate death. But if we had not found them, they would not have survived either, and would have died a slow lingering cruel death of starvation and thirst in the bush. At least we had tried to save them.

Working with wild buffalo will humble a man. I have witnessed the raw mighty power of an angry rampaging bull and have seen two cows savagely fight to the death in 'The Buffalo Fight Club', and it makes me realise how fragile and puny we humans are compared to them. But I have also seen the softer side of these magnificent wild beasts, where a cow trusted me enough to eat lucerne out of my hand, and a young bull, who could crush me like an insect, licked my hand like a puppy dog. I consider it an honour and a privilege to have been given the opportunity to witness these things, and none of this would have happened if I had not put the Law of Attraction into action and moved out from Durban! *If nothing changes, then nothing changes, and everything remains the same!* But, when you find the courage to make that change, an amazing adventure beyond what you thought or asked, will unfold before you! Make the change!

All that was left to do was to instruct our driver to get the JCB excavator and dig a big deep hole near where they had fallen and bury them. While I went back to my house where I emailed the boss and explained how he had just lost a million rands worth of buffalo. The only upside was that he still had 48 buffalo left, and next year's calves would replace the loss. But still that was not compensation enough for the loss of two magnificent beasts! I sat outside that evening under a clear, star-filled sky and contemplated how quickly things could change. Soon my thought turned to my own future. It is amazing how decisions made in solitude and quietness turn out to be the right decisions. My situation was, that my age and a few medical conditions were impacting my ability to effectively manage the ranch. But what did I have to work with? The only logical answer was to resign and move back to England. I did not relish the idea of the long cold dark winters, but I had worked in England some years before and knew this would entitle me to claim a pension. There was also free medical and several other benefits, such as housing that I could claim. Also, my daughter and a few of my relatives had already moved there, so I would have their help and support. In England I could survive comfortably in my mature years, and I would have family around me. I could now retire completely. Whereas in South Africa I could have quite easily landed up on the streets with no support. My time on the ranch was a wonderful end to my working career, the best job I ever had! *Fortune favours the brave, and to the victor, the spoils!* Be bold! Take a blind step in faith, and you will be amazed where it leads you. Hoist your sail, and let the wind take you where it will!

Porcupine pie

The boss had one more thing he wanted me to do. He wanted to update his big garden with indigenous plants, and I knew a lady who specialised in indigenous gardens and had transformed a few other wildlife resorts. I called her in, and she submitted a quote, which was quite substantial, but the boss accepted it and soon she was on site with her crew with loads of plants and began work. After a few days' work she arrived at the ranch in the morning, and I heard her let out an alarmed yell! I ran to see what was up, and she showed me that all the succulent wild aloe plants that she had planted out had been eaten overnight right down to the roots! That was bad news as she would have to replace them. But next morning all the aloes she had replaced had also been eaten. There is only one animal that loves aloes and that is the porcupine, and he had to be stopped!

I borrowed an animal trap from a friend and set it up where we thought he was coming on to the property, but days went by, and he evaded the trap and continued gorging himself on newly planted aloes. Much to our frustration. Then one evening as I sat in my house watching TV, the porcupine as bold as brass, strolled past the big glass doors on my deck and happily helped himself to the leftover dog food in the bowls on the deck. Bloody cheek I call it! I jumped up from my chair and he immediately did an about turn and disappeared off the deck into the bush. Next evening, I was waiting for him, and kept the light out in the lounge so he couldn't see me. Right on time he came strolling across the deck and started snacking on the dog food. Very quietly I got up from my chair with my .38 Spl revolver in hand and sneaked out the back door and came up behind him. Immediately he became aware of me he turned towards me and charged! Fearful of his long needle-sharp quills I instinctively took aim and fired at the middle of his back when he was no less than three paces from me. But it didn't even slow him down, and he ran past me on my left! In disbelief I spun around and fired a second shot into his back, but he just continued running and disappeared off the side of the deck and into the night! I stood there dumbfounded! How could I have missed! I can hit beer cans easily at ten paces! But if I had missed there would be bullet holes in the wooden deck, and I couldn't see any!

Next morning, I examined the deck carefully, and could not find any bullet holes! Herein was a mystery! Then I noticed a mark in the wall on the far side that hadn't been there before, and on closer examination I found it to be bullet shrapnel. Not a full bullet embedded in the wall, just bits of brass jacket shrapnel. From this I concluded the bullets had bounced harmlessly off the thick armour of his long quills and hit the wall and allowed him to escape. Tough little buggers these porcupines! So, we brought the trap and placed it near my back door and baited it with some nice juicy pumpkin, and that did the trick! Next morning the trap was sprung and inside was a full-grown male porcupine. He turned his back on me as I approached the trap and rattled his long sharp quills at me in a defiant warning. In the middle of his back there was a big patch where the quills were missing. Damaged quills are pushed out by the porcupine and new ones soon grow it their place. I had not missed! We loaded the trap on to my pickup and I took him 20 miles away on to the other side of a river and let him go near another wildlife resort. I decided not to make porcupine pie out of him. He had survived two slugs from a powerful .38 Spl handgun and deserved to live.

The boss and his wife returned two weeks later from their wandering to and fro upon the face of the Earth and were well pleased with the revamp of the garden, especially all the aloes that had caused us so much grief. Later I sat down with them and discussed my decision to leave. They were disappointed but thanked me for my honesty instead of trying to hide it in order to hang on to my job. A date was now set for my departure from the ranch, and it was with much sadness that I said my final goodbyes to the staff who had worked so well with me, and to the boss and his wife and all the wild animals on the ranch. As a parting gift I gave the boss and his wife a big painting of a lion I had done several years before, and they hung it in pride of place over the fireplace in their lounge. As I left the gates of the ranch for the last time a beautiful chapter of my life closed behind me, and a new chapter was about to begin. This time I was not faced with an uncertain future, or not knowing what lay ahead. I could face the future with confidence.

My goals for England remained the same as the ones I set on the way down from Durban. A good place to stay. A sustainable income, and a good car to drive, and I *knew* without a shadow of a doubt that I would get what I Asked for, because I <u>KNOW</u> The Law of Attraction works!

Chapter 4

England!

As I already had British citizenship because my dad came from a long line of ancestors in England, all I had to do was book my seat on a plane and I could fly away. But I was not prepared to leave my dog behind. So began the task of getting her vaccinated for British requirements to import her and organising with a pet carrier firm to transport her over. I would have to leave her in South Africa for the quarantine period required by England and I knew she would pine for me, so I asked my mate to look after her on the farm. In all it cost me a lot more to put her in a pet box in the hold of the aircraft than the comfortable seat I had inside the cabin. Fortunately, my time on the wildlife ranch had built up my bank balance considerably and I could well afford it. No more having to rely on handouts or charity!

The day came for my departure, and I said my goodbyes to my friend David and his family and went to the airport, only to find the travel agent had neglected to inform me that the departure time had been changed and when I got to the airport the plane was long gone and I had to rebook a flight out the next day, which of course cost extra. Very annoying as I had to spend another night in a hotel, but I made sure I was back at the airport the next day on time and took off and winged my way to England and a new chapter in my life.

Landing at Heathrow airport I did not have to join the long queues of tourists at the immigration desk and was ushered into the short returning citizen's queue. There I was greeted by a black British customs' officer who examined my passport and handed it back to me saying, in a very British accent, "Alright mate, welcome 'ome." It seemed strange to me, and sort of didn't quite fit as I was only used to the black South African accent! I smiled broadly and thanked him and walked into England. It was like coming home. My dad had left England in 1920 and never returned and now I was completing the circle. All my ancestors and history are in England. I was born British, yet just not in England, but in the then British colony of Rhodesia. I was met by my daughter who had moved to England some years before. She had agreed to take care of me until I got my pension and housing sorted, so I lived at her place in Yorkshire for the next three months.

I eventually got my pension sorted which was adequate to live on with a bit to spare. I was granted housing allowance and was offered a studio flat in a sheltered housing complex full of mature people my age. The flat was small but because I was single, I was not eligible for a one-bedroom flat. I immediately got myself an easel, oil paints and brushes and began to paint pictures. This helped me settle into England as it takes some adjusting and getting used to. I had never worked in oils before, so it was a new learning curve for me, but I quickly got the hang of it and was turning out some good paintings. This soon became known around the complex and people were eager to see what I painted next. I painted 20 pictures in the next year. The residents were a friendly crowd, and I soon had a bunch of friends around me. The time came for my dog to arrive in England and one of the ladies offered to drive me to Heathrow to collect her. When my dog walked through the airport doors, she spotted me immediately and went nuts! It was a very happy reunion with her jumping up and down and wagging her little stump of a tail till I thought it would fall off! All the way home she sat on my lap and smothered my face in kisses from her little wet tongue! I couldn't be happier! My mate in South Africa told me how she would sit by the gate on the farm all day and look up the road hoping for my return. If any vehicles came to the farm, she would run over to them hoping I was there, and when I wasn't there, she would return to her spot by the gate and sit there looking up the road.

Life settled into a routine. I was content with my life. I had a nice place to stay in, and friends around me. I had enough money to live on and after about a year I saved enough to buy myself a small car. The first one I could buy in over 15 years! The darn thing nearly got me killed about a year later when it suffered a sudden mechanical failure on a very busy two-lane motorway on a wet and misty day, and I nearly got wiped out from behind by a line of big heavy-duty trucks doing 70 miles an hour which missed me by inches. Scary stuff! But I had achieved the three goals I had set for England, good housing, enough money to live on, and a car. For this I am extremely grateful! Again, I had made the change, I asked for what I wanted, believed that I would receive, and it worked out for the good. I also had a miracle take place with my car. It suffered a mechanical failure that would have cost more than the car was worth to repair and

I was offered £100 as scrap value for it. But the lady who lived two doors down from me had just bought herself a new car and had been offered £100 scrap value for her little green Fiesta, which I knew was in good working order. So, I sold my car for £100 which I gave to the lady for her car and drove the little green car for the next three years without a moments problem, until it got eaten up with rust on the undercarriage and failed the M.O.T. roadworthy test. It was far more than the value of the car to make it worthwhile repairing. More about the miracle that took place with my next car later. What you ask for, you get! Thoughts become things. The Law of Attraction works!

After two years my daughter took a job near London, and I moved to Windsor to be near her. Again, I was offered a small studio flat in a sheltered housing complex. I found Windsor too crowded and jammed full of tourists, all coming to see the castle and ride the tour boats up and down the Thames River. I loved walking my dog along the banks and through its parks and got to go and see the inside of Windsor Castle which was amazing. But I found Windsor to be unfriendly, especially where I lived. Nobody made any attempt to welcome me or make friends with me, so I largely stayed it my flat for three years and painted pictures till I had no more space on my wall to hang them. Even though I gave a number of them to my daughter to hang in her flat. Besides that, because of the Covid 19 pandemic I was self-isolating for over a year and a half and was suffering from cabin fever. So, in all I did not enjoy my stay in Windsor and was unhappy there.

But it was here one day as I was browsing through Amazon, the title of a book stood out and I felt strangely drawn to it. It had a big old fashioned red wax seal on it with the words written across it, *The Secret*, by Rhonda Byrne. I was intrigued, it was like I had to know what this secret was. On the back cover I read, *'As you learn The Secret, you will come to know how you can have, be, or do anything you want.'* I guess that because I was unhappy in the situation in Windsor that I ordered a copy. When the book arrived, I immediately sat down to read it. I was amazed to find it was based on the Bible verse, **Mark 11:24**. *'Whatever you desire, when you pray, believe that you receive, and you shall have it.'* The Secret does not portray this as a Spiritual Law or anything religious, but shows it to be a natural law, the Law of Attraction, which I had already been using for years. It is dependent on the power of belief, your faith, to attract to yourself the things you desire! Everybody has the natural ability to Believe, we are all born with a measure of Faith. Did you believe you could learn to drive a car or ride a push bike? I was already using many of the principles outlined in the book, such as visualisation and affirmations to reach the goals I set for myself. I just didn't know I was using the Law of Attraction, so I set myself to learn more about it. I introduced the book to my daughter, who immediately saw the value in it and began to put it into practice.

From reading The Secret, I began to realise I had settled for having just enough to live on with a little to spare. I was content to live in a small studio flat, drive a small car, and have just enough to live on, when I could raise my sights and have Abundant Living! There are no limits! So, I changed my goals and affirmations to include a better lifestyle. I decided I would Ask for my own property. I wanted space around me, and set the goal of a property in a rural area with a few acres of land around me. I visualised the type of house I wanted to live in, an old character-style farmhouse. I set the figure for the income I wanted, and I would need the interest from investments to achieve this. For the vehicle I wanted to drive, I set my sights on a vehicle I had always wanted. An old Chilli Red X-type Jaguar 3L automatic from about 2007. At the time I set these goals there was no way I could achieve them on the income I was receiving. I would need another miracle! I don't just believe in miracles, now I depend on them!

As I have said, the Law of Attraction is like magnetism. Any thought or desires you hold strongly in your mind will be attracted to you, and you will have them! The key comes in the words, 'effectual, fervent prayer,' or Asking. If there is 'effectual' prayer, then there is also 'ineffectual' prayer. This is meaningless vain repetition. Even saying the Lord's Prayer over and over again is meaningless repetition as it was never meant to be a magic blanket to cover all circumstances. It is a guide to what things you need to ask for, individually! Then there is the word, 'fervent'. This is not wishy-washy, ask once and forget it type asking. It involves emotion. A strong determination. A stubborn refusal to give up until you get what you want. It also takes practise, and the more you practise, the easier it becomes!

It was my daughter again who brought about the change. She got a good job down in the old market town of Petersfield, which is not far from Portsmouth, and needed to move there. We began looking around in the area for a place for myself as she wanted me near her so she could help me when I needed it. Each place that catered for my needs had a long waiting list or did not allow dogs. The search went on for some time, and each time we came up empty. Then out of the blue we got a call from a place we had only phoned once, and I received an invite to come and look at a one-bedroom flat in a nice, sheltered housing complex. A one-bedroom flat? Where all I had been offered elsewhere was a studio flat! There were five other people waiting in line and I had first choice! So, I had to move fast! My daughter and I made an appointment to view the flat, and on the day, we were greeted by some of the residents who were very friendly, one came from Rhodesia, and another came from South Africa. That was a good start. I felt positive about the place from the beginning. The grounds were three times bigger than Windsor with lovely gardens and open dog walking parks nearby. The town centre was five minutes down the road. Petersfield is a rural town, uncluttered and open, which suited me fine. The complex manageress showed us the flat and the first surprise was that it had a remote-controlled front door! The inside was far bigger than the small studio flat I was in. It was freshly painted and of course had a separate bedroom. Furthermore, it was a £100 cheaper than Windsor! The manageress started to say, "Now *if* you want the flat…" And I cut her short, "What do you mean *IF*?" I asked with a smile. "I want the flat, I'll take it!" So began the move to Petersfield and a much happier life than I had in Windsor. I had not specifically asked for anything for my new flat but had an idea in my mind as to what I would like. This was enough to attract to me what I wanted, and this flat certainty ticked all the boxes! Including the remote-controlled door! Which was just a thought at the time. Thoughts held firmly in your mind become reality! Be warned, that applies to wrong thoughts just as effectively!

Once I had settled into the new flat, I began to seriously concentrate on the new goals I had set for myself. Each day I fervently visualised them and repeated the affirmations I had written out for the new goals. There was no doubt in my mind that I would have what I Asked for! At this time the yearly M.O.T. (roadworthy test) came up for my little green Fiesta. She had served me well and was mechanically sound, but the bodywork was full of rust and one door hinge would need replacing which was a big cut and weld job. She failed the M.O.T. and would cost more than the car was worth to repair. I decided it was time for her to retire. Now was the right time for the X-type Jag to come into being, and I began to look for one. It was my daughter who found one online up in Birmingham at a very good price below £2000. At least a thousand less that I had seen other X-type Jags advertised for. We contacted the dealer and got pictures of the car which I scrutinised. I determined she was mechanically sound but not in perfect condition and just needed some TLC. The car was everything I wanted, Chilli Red in colour, automatic, leather seats, but a 2.5L engine not 3L, and a 2006 model, not 2007, as I had first envisioned. But I decided that was close enough. I organised a loan with the bank and my daughter and I went up to Birmingham to look at it. After looking the car over I felt positive this was the one and bought it. It was a dream come true! I had never thought that I would own a Jag, and now I do! When we got back to Petersfield, I parked her in the spot where I had parked the Fiesta and couldn't stop looking at her! The feeling I got was overwhelming, I had Asked for an X-type Jag, and now that Ask was reality! I almost felt afraid to take her out on the road and drive her, in case some other silly uninsured driver smashed into her! It did take a while for it to sink in that I own a Chilli Red X-type Jag! I still look at it and say, "Thank you Lord for my Jag!" It is always important to give thanks and exercise the Attitude of Gratitude once you have received what you have Asked for.

Of course, for the two remaining goals I would need money, and I didn't have much of that. So, I began to ask, 'How do I get the money I need?' As I mulled this over in my mind,

I began to think as I did in Port Alfred. 'What do I have to work with? What can I use?' In Port Alfred I had all the experience and guns I needed for farm-sitting, but that wouldn't work in England. They certainly don't like guns here! Then it came to me, I have a story to tell. A story that can also help other people who find themselves in The Valley of the Shadow. A story that, if they just apply the principals involved as I did, will get them out onto the plains of the Serengeti, as it did for me. A place of peace and abundant living, where you can have whatsoever things you desire! *If nothing changes, then nothing changes, and everything remains the same!* Mine has been an incredible journey. I have written a few stories for magazines in the past and had them published, So, why not write a book?! The royalties from the book could pay for the two remaining goals. The fact that you are reading this book today means you are contributing to the fulfilment of those last two goals, and what I have asked for, and believe that I already have, I will get! I want to thank you all for your help, and I hope this story will help you, whatever situation you are in. Dare to take a blind leap in faith but be prepared to tough it out and stubbornly see it through, and you will get whatever you desire, and get out of your Valley of The Shadow!

About the Author

Jon was born in old British Colonial Southern Rhodesia in Africa, which is now called Zimbabwe. His father was the reduction officer on a small gold mine, 10 miles out in the bush near the town of Hartley. It was his father's job to help run the mine and to smelt down the gold into gold bars about the size of a brick at the end of the month. Young Jon often got to see the end products of a few bright shiny gold bars on the table in the manager's office. He had 2 sisters, both older than him, and there were not many other white families on the mine and only a few other children to play with, so his early years were lonely. Especially when his sisters went off to boarding school. When his time came, he followed his sisters to boarding school many miles from home and was away for 3 months at a time, and so was deprived of a loving home environment up bringing. Jon hated boarding school and it soon emerged that he had a learning disability in that he is dyslexic, a condition where letters and numbers get mixed up in the brain, and spelling and doing sums become a nightmare. The teachers, not knowing any better, just called him stupid. It also emerged later that he is somewhat red – green colour blind. His years at junior school were very unhappy and he was bullied because he was the small skinny little kid and considered to be stupid. Yet, despite the cards being stacked against him as a kid, Jon in his adult years overcame these obstacles. His attitude is you only have 3 choices in life. 'Improvise, adapt, or overcome!' It is not what life throws at you that counts, it is how you react to it! Today Jon is an author, thanks to computers that handle the spelling. He has written several articles for magazines, and this is his first book. Jon is a self-taught artist and paints wildlife, seascapes, and landscapes. He is also a self-taught mechanic, and he learned to play the guitar. He was a lay preacher in his church for 7 years before he retired. This required 2 years of theological studies, and he passed the exams with flying colours. A far cry from his school years! Jon's attitude to life is that a person can overcome any obstacle in life, any difficulty or disability, if they put their mind to it and learn how to use the natural and spiritual laws of life that are available to them! You can get out of The Valley of the Shadow!